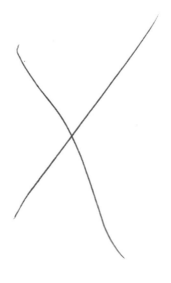

To my parents, with love

MAKE YOUR OWN
CURTAINS & BLINDS

LANI VAN REENEN

PHOTOGRAPHS BY ALAIN PROUST AND JUAN ESPI
ILLUSTRATIONS BY JANE FENEMORE

NEW
HOLLAND

First published in the UK in 1993 by
New Holland (Publishers) Ltd
37 Connaught Street, London W2 2AZ

ISBN 1-85368-269-1

Editor: Linda de Villiers
Designer: Janice Evans
Photographers: Alain Proust and Juan Espi
Illustrations: Jane Fenemore

Typesetting by Diatype Setting CC
Reproduction by Unifoto (Pty) Ltd
Printed and bound in Singapore by Kyodo Printing Co
Singapore (Pte) Ltd

ACKNOWLEDGEMENTS
The publishers would like to thank Pru Pfuhl and the Biggie Best
chain of interior decorating shops for their help in creating this book.

For further details of Biggie Best's wide range of fabrics and
accessories, please contact in the UK:

Biggie Best
109-111 South Liberty Lane
Ashton Vale Trading Estate
Bristol
Fax: (0272) 53-5588

In Australia:
Biggie Best
6A Lakeway
Claremont
Perth
Western Australia
Fax: (09) 385-2140

One of the Biggie Best stores housed in a building
reminiscent of the Victorian era.

CONTENTS

PREFACE

For the past ten years I have been closely involved with the home décor business and also with doing up my own home. During this time I have come to realise the need for a practical guide to window decorating. In this book I have attempted to give guidelines to window-dressing in general and clear instructions on how to 'do-it-yourself'. I hope the book will also serve as a source of inspiration, so that when paging through it, you will become excited at the prospect of revamping the 'tired' areas of your home and by the idea of developing your own unique style of window decoration.

OPPOSITE: A pretty clutter of gifts and decorating accessories, which proved an invaluable source of inspiration in the creation of the blind and curtain designs presented in the following pages.

INTRODUCTION

One of the most important features of any room is its windows. They perform many crucial functions including allowing air to circulate in summer, keeping out bad weather in winter, and letting in light and providing a link with the outside world all year round. Frequently they also form an integral part of the architectural style of a room, provide a focal point, or stand as attractive features in their own right.

For a variety of reasons such as privacy, insulation or perhaps the disguise of a less than attractive outlook, virtually all windows need to be 'dressed'. So often, however, this wonderful opportunity for creative decorating remains unexplored to its full potential. In this book, therefore, we aim to show you how to revolutionize this important aspect of your home and how to make the very most of your windows.

With practical and aesthetic considerations given equal emphasis, in no time at all you will be able to embark on planning imaginative and successful design schemes and on making up your own curtains and blinds in true professional fashion.

Selecting the right covering

Choosing the most appropriate type of covering for a window involves several major considerations, not least of which are the shape and style of the window in question. Its position within a room, its function and the role it can play in the overall decorating plan are just as important.

Full guidance is given on how to assess these factors in relation to a wide variety of window types, including arches, bows, dormers, French windows, and long, narrow, short and wide windows. Decorating solutions, colour schemes and fabric designs are discussed in detail, as well as how best to make the important decision of whether to opt for curtains or blinds.

Once the creative planning stages for your new window décor have been accomplished, the practicalities of acquiring materials and making up must be addressed. To ensure really successful results, it is always worth taking trouble over the details: careful measuring up, the choice of rods, tracks and so forth, and the correct use of lining materials are all relevant to getting the best results. So too is the right type of fabric: quality medium-weight cotton is recommended as a good general purpose window-dressing fabric and it predominates in the designs chosen for this book. Among its numerous advantages are the fact that it is simple to care for, is easily lined, hangs well and can be dressed 'up' (with

ABOVE: Examples of the wide choice of colour co-ordinated fabrics available today.
OPPOSITE: Antique lace draped over curtain poles softens the stark lines of two identical Roman blinds.

Pretty and informal in candy-pink, with frills on the curtains, valances and tie-backs.

swags and bows for a grand effect) or 'down' (for a more casual, cottagey feel). To help overcome any potential pitfalls, full instructions are given on all the technical aspects of making up the widest possible range of curtain and blind styles, and indeed the decorations with which well-executed 'accessories', such as bows, swags, rosettes and tie-backs, can make all the difference to the final result.

Bows are used to focus attention on certain areas of the window dressing, and to provide interesting touches to blinds, valances and tie-backs. Swags and tails can be used as an alternative to curtains if your window is asymmetrical, while tie-backs will immediately let more light into your room if the window is small. They also provide the ultimate finishing touch to your curtains if the same fabric is used. Instruc-

The Jacobean design in maroon and navy against shirt-stripe wallpaper creates a sophisticated look.

tions on choosing the correct 'accessories' for your window are given throughout the book. By adding these final touches you can easily transform any room, and make it appear formal, or elegant, or dramatic, depending on the effect you wish to create.

So if you are enthused by the prospect of giving a fresh and imaginative look to the windows of your home, plan to embark on a whole new decorating scheme, or are simply looking for the best way to dress a difficult window, we hope you will find the answers here. Once the basics have been mastered and a few of the simpler projects completed, you will discover just how enjoyable and rewarding creative window-dressing can be and there will be no limit to the decorative heights you can reach.

CHAPTER ONE
WINDOWS

The windows of a house are the point of contact between the inner personal, intimate and private living space and the outside world. Windows also allow air, light, heat or cold to enter the living space. In order to ensure privacy, prevent glare, insulate, and sometimes to hide an unattractive view, it is essential that windows are 'dressed'. These practical considerations provide a wonderful opportunity for creative interior decorating; after all, window-dressing is one of the most important aspects of a room.

The traditional paisley design in maroon and navy sets a formal atmosphere. A double row of pencil pleat tape is used to create the curtain heading.

A specific architectural style and period is incorporated into every home, and this will largely determine the style of window-dressing. For example, a formal room with large windows will require full-length curtains in plain colours or a subdued, striped design, with a formal pelmet and tie-backs. On the other hand, a cheerful curtain in a floral pattern in the cottagey style, complete with frills and valance, would be the better choice for a smaller window in an informal room. Most shops offer you suitable fabrics for both options.

Some windows have unattractive angular lines which may be softened and disguised by curtains that completely cover the windows, while others might have such an attractive frame and architrave that the window-dressing should accentuate and draw attention to these features. Windows that have been positioned in a room in order to show off a beautiful view to best advantage should be treated with sensitivity and creativity so that the dressing will emphasize rather than detract from this aspect.

The atmosphere or mood of a room is greatly affected by the quality, strength and diffusion of natural light. This should be borne in mind when choosing a style, as well as when selecting the colour and design of the fabric for the windows of your home.

The window-dressing is an integral part of the decorative impact of a room. It can be the focal point around which other features are planned, or it can provide a subtle backdrop to enhance other dynamic aspects of the room's décor, for example furniture or paintings. Whatever the style – whether formal or informal, restful or cheerful, elegant or cottagey – there are choices of curtains or blinds which will reflect these qualities.

It is important to make a critical assessment of the proportions and sizes of the windows in relation to the rest of the room. By intelligent 'placing' of the window-dressing, such proportions may be changed to create illusions of higher, lower, larger or smaller windows.

Long, narrow windows

It will not always be necessary to attempt to change the proportions/sizes of the windows. In old houses we often find beautiful wooden sash windows and architraves, and in order to emphasize these features, a Roman or festoon blind within the window reveal is a good choice.

Where a window has no particular redeeming feature and is too narrow in relation to the surrounding wall space, an illusion of a larger window may be created by placing a curtain

The height of the tall windows has been visually reduced by a full valance *(left)*, while the height of the window *(above)* lends itself to the rather heavy treatment of two curtains, hung one behind the other.

track or rod directly above the window and allowing it to extend some distance beyond the edges. The new width is hung with full-length curtains which are tied back to the edge of the window frame during the day. This admits the maximum amount of light. A pelmet or gathered valance will reduce the apparent height of the window. This should be placed right above the window and must be deep enough to enclose a part of the window at the top.

Short, wide windows

Place the curtain track or rod well above the window frame, and use full-length curtains. Disguise the track with a deep pelmet, gathered valance or swag and tails which cover the top part of the window. In order to make the excess width less conspicuous, the curtains may be permanently attached to each other at the centre-point of the track or rod, and then tied back during the day *(see Fig. 1)*.

A café-curtain, hung on a brass rod placed just above a window-sill and hanging quite far below the sill, and a deep valance will also create the illusion of a larger window. The café-curtain and valance are permanent fixtures and are therefore never opened or closed *(see Fig. 2)*.

BELOW: A café curtain ensures privacy by covering this bathroom window to eye level while, at the same time, letting in light through the top.
OPPOSITE: A Roman blind is teamed with a heavy mock festoon valance and mock curtains, which visually alter the proportions of the window.

Fig. 1

Fig. 2

Two or more windows in one wall

If the windows are close together, they should be treated as a single unit by using a single curtain track or rod. During the day, full-length curtains may be opened all the way, provided there is enough wall space to accommodate them. Alternatively, while still sharing a track, each window may have its own pair of curtains which, when drawn back during the day, will occupy the wall space to the sides and between the windows. The same principle applies in the case of a glass door and a window which are close together in a single wall.

The problem of asymmetrical windows may be solved by using a deep pelmet or valance to bring the height of the windows into line. Full-length curtains will disguise any height differences between the window and the floor *(see Fig. 3)*.

However, if the windows are symmetrical and there is a reasonable space between them, it is better to deal with them individually, provided they are treated in a similar way. The wall space in between is ideal for paintings, a decorative table, a standing lamp or an attractive chair or settee.

Fig. 3

BELOW: Identical swags and tails have been used as the only decoration on this pair of sash windows positioned next to one another in the same wall.

A single window in the corner of a room

A problem arises when there is little or no wall space next to a window in the corner of a room, and where conventional curtains cannot be drawn back equally to either side of the window. One solution is to make a single curtain which can be either draped to one side with a tie-back *(see Fig. 4)* or tied in the centre with a decorative bow during the day *(see Fig. 5)*. Another alternative is a Roman or ruched blind (Austrian or festoon) because this can be pulled up uniformly.

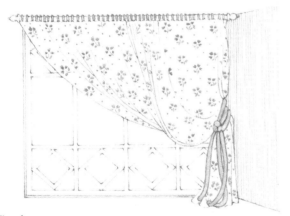

Fig. 4

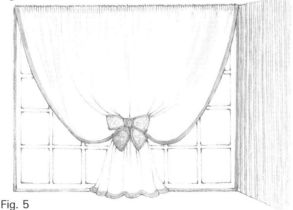

Fig. 5

Two windows on either side of the corner of a room

Windows may meet in the corner or may come very close to the corner. A solution here is a continuous curtain track which curves around the corner.

A single curtain can be made for each window and may be drawn or tied back to the furthest point during the day. This ensures an uninterrupted view and admits the maximum amount of light. Each window can also have a pair of curtains. During the day the two curtains that are closest to the corner may be drawn or tied back to the corner, and the other two to the furthest points.

If you wish to emphasize the unity of the windows even more and at the same time disguise the curtain track, a pelmet may be made to fit into the corner, or a valance may be hung around the corner on a double track.

In the case of short windows with windowsills, Roman or ruched blinds may be used to good effect.

The valance and curtains hang from a double track that was bent to fit into the corner.

Bay windows

A bay window with its angular proportions and beautiful wooden sash windows is a great asset in a room, and these features should be emphasized by the window-dressing. Where windows rest on a windowsill and thus don't occupy the full height of the wall, built-in upholstered seating can be designed to fit exactly into the bay. Attractively strewn with scatter cushions, it provides extra seating in the room and turns the bay window into a cosy focal point. Curtains or blinds should extend only down to the windowsill. If you use blinds, these should be made for each individual window. Full length mock (dummy) curtains on either side of the win-

dow look very attractive with the blinds. If curtains are your preference, the curtain track should follow the lines and angles of the bay window and each window should have its own curtain, that is, one curtain for each outside window and two for the central window. During the day, each of the four curtains is tied back to the nearest window frame. This treatment also applies to bay windows which occupy the full height of the wall and where curtains therefore extend to the floor. Blinds should not be used in this case.

If appropriate to the height of the windows, a sculpted pelmet, valance or mock festoon valance or swags and tails may be added to the curtains.

Formal swags and tails and full-length curtains decorate this bay window *(below)*, while informal festoon blinds hang over a built-in bay seat *(opposite)* to create a cosy focal point.

Very large windows

Windows which occupy a large proportion of the height and width of a wall are best served by full-length curtains. If there is a large sliding door or window, it is important to ensure that access through the door is not obstructed by the curtains. It is advisable to extend the curtain track beyond the windows so that the large volume of fabric can be drawn or tied back into the wall space beside the window during the day. If the large window consists of panels, individual pairs of curtains may be made for each panel and tied back during the day to the frames which separate the panels. As a great deal of heat may be lost through large windows, particularly during the cold months, it is advisable to interline the curtains to provide better insulation.

To facilitate easy access, these full curtains are tied back during the day in the wall space beside the sliding door.

French windows (doors)

What is meant here are wooden or metal doors with glass panels which open inwards or outwards. Sometimes there are also windows above and on either side of the doors, all within the same frame. These door-windows are very attractive and often add a great deal to the general atmosphere of a room: they can be left, therefore, in their 'undressed' state, provided this does not mean a loss of privacy.

If French windows must be covered, it is important that they should be able to open and close without difficulty. If there is enough space on either side, the curtain track or rod may again extend beyond the frame of the doors so that curtains can be drawn or tied back completely during the day.

French doors *(right)* opening to the outside are dressed with a valance, curtains and festoon blind. Curtains on cased headings are used on the French doors that open to the inside *(below)*.

Where there is a window above the French windows, a Roman blind is an attractive option as it may be pulled up into this space above the door, allowing the doors to open and close freely.

Another alternative is to make blinds which are attached to the doors themselves, and which then move with the doors when they open or close.

Dormer windows

These are small windows placed in a sloping roof and are mostly found in bedrooms on the top storey or in the attic of a house. Because these windows are small, the window-dressing should be such as to admit the maximum amount of light. Two possibilities are narrow curtains, which can be tied back during the day, or frilled curtains which can be tied back to the upper edges of the window *(see Fig. 6)*.

Another creative solution is to gather the curtain on a rod which opens and closes with a swivelling action so that the curtains may be swung away from the window and tied back if necessary. This ensures privacy at night and maximum light during the day *(see Fig. 7)*.

A Roman blind, which can be pulled up to occupy very little space, may be used, and where the size of the window makes it possible, a ruched blind looks lovely.

The principles used for dormer windows may also be applied to other small and sometimes inconspicuous windows, giving them significance within the total decorating scheme of a room.

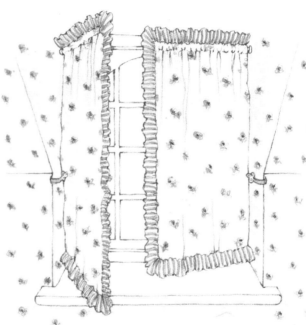

Fig. 7

a swivel rod

OPPOSITE: A pretty picture is created in this dormer window with frilled curtains, a pelmet and wallpaper in a medley of roses and stripes.

Fig. 6

Arched windows

An arched window looks so attractive in a room that it should not be obscured. If possible, the window should not be covered at all, but if curtains do seem necessary, they should hang from a rod placed far above the window, and extend well beyond the frame. During the day, when curtains have been opened, the frame will thus be fully exposed. A smaller arched window is enhanced by a ruched blind suspended from an arched track. On a large arched window, an arched track may be installed from which full-length curtains can hang. When calculating the amount of fabric required, bear in mind that the length is measured from the centre of the arch. Gather the fabric to the required finished width, and then cut away the excess fabric to follow the curve of the arch.

Treatment for a long arched window can consist of a pelmet which is arched along its bottom edge and, therefore, follows the shape of the arch without obscuring it.

An attractive festoon blind is installed within the reveal of the arched window *(left)* while full-length curtains hang from an arched track *(above)*.

Windows that should not be dressed

Window-dressing softens the hard, angular lines of windows. However, in some instances the windows have been architecturally designed for aesthetic rather than functional purposes and as such should not be covered.

Some older houses have windows with such lovely proportions and beautiful wooden frames that it would be a pity to cover them, unless absolutely necessary. Sometimes all that is needed to ensure privacy are shutters, which can be painted or left in their natural state.

Undressed windows may be decorated by painting the window frames in interesting contrasting colours. If the window does not have an architrave, a wallpaper border may be used for decoration around the window.

LEFT: Two matching designs of wallpaper borders create a stunning effect around this window.

ABOVE: The stained glass window on this staircase is a magnificent feature of a Victorian house and should be left unadorned. The coloured glass panels ensure privacy.

CHAPTER TWO
CURTAINS

*When curtains are the right choice for the windows
that you want to 'dress', and you have decided to
make them yourself, the following practical
guidelines and information will be helpful.*

The track or rod from which curtains are hung will determine to a large extent the style of the curtains. A curtain rod, whether of wood or brass, is decorative and should be displayed. A track, on the other hand, should always be covered by a curtain heading. The method of hanging the curtain, either on a rod or a track, will in turn determine the choice of the curtain heading.

Curtain tracks

Curtain tracks may be plastic for light-weight curtains or metal for medium- or heavy-weight ones. The track comes complete with runners that have eyelets through which the hooks of the curtain heading are passed, as well as wall brackets. Some wall brackets are expandable so that the space between the wall and the track may be adjusted. This type of mounting bracket is useful when there is a blind behind the curtain or when the track must extend beyond a wooden window frame.

If a valance is to be used with a curtain, a double track is mounted on special wall brackets. In this case, ensure that the light-weight track is placed in front and the heavy-weight track at the back.

Tracks can be bent according to the shape of the window, for example in the curved shape of a bay window or around the arch of an arched window.

As mentioned earlier, different effects can be achieved by the positioning of the curtain track. Generally, however, the track should extend sufficiently on both sides of the window so that the fullness of the opened curtains can be accommodated in the wall space beside the window. This also allows the maximum amount of light to enter during the day.

The height of the track above the window will depend on the proportion of each window to its wall space. Usually 10-15 cm is sufficient. If the window is near the ceiling, the track should be mounted as close to the cornice as possible so that that section of the wall will be covered by the curtain.

A plastic track for light-weight curtains

An aluminium track for medium- and heavy-weight curtains

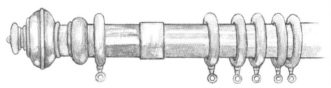

A double track for curtains and a valance

A brass curtain rod and rings

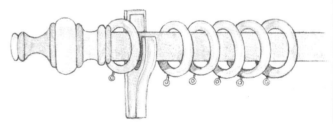

A wooden curtain rod and rings

Tracks with a cord system for opening and closing curtains prevent them from becoming hand-soiled. Draw-sticks which, together with the inner hook on each pair of curtains, are hung from the eyes of the two central runners, may also be used for this purpose. Also available is the overlap runner, which allows the two inner edges of the curtains to overlap by a few centimetres at the centre of the track.

Curtain rods

Curtain rods are made of wood or brass and, apart from their functional purpose, are part of the window decoration. Each large curtain ring on the rod is fitted with a screw eye from which the hooks on the curtain heading are suspended. Curtain rods are supported by brackets, and the curtains are fixed on the rod at their outer edges by positioning the outermost rings beyond the brackets on either side. Rods are usually placed 15-20 cm above a window.

Curtain headings

Curtains hang from the track or rod by curtain hooks that have been pulled through the pockets on the heading tape which is stitched to the upper edge of the curtain and creates the decorative heading once it has been gathered. Various types of heading tape are available and these determine the style of the curtain, that is, formal or informal. Heading tape is available in nylon for light-weight curtains and in cotton for heavier ones. The gathering width of the curtain will also be dependent on the type of heading tape used.

Gathered pleats

The heading tape for gathered pleats is the narrowest, has a single row of suspension pockets and is gathered by means of two pull-strings to form a shallow curtain heading. This heading is suitable for informal and unlined curtains in a bathroom or kitchen for example. An attractive frill to cover the curtain track can be obtained by attaching the tape a few centimetres below the top of the curtain. This narrow heading tape is also suitable for curtains hanging behind a pelmet or valance. The gathering width is usually twice the length of the curtain track.

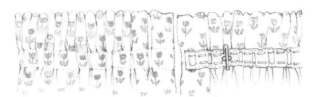

Gathered pleats

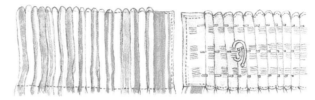

Pencil pleats

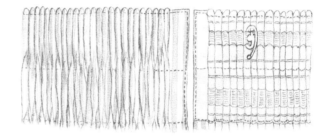

Pencil pleats (special tape for a smocked effect)

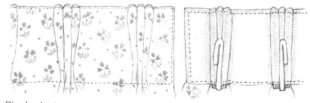

Pinch pleats

Pencil pleats

This heading tape is broad and is gathered by means of two or three pull-strings to form neat, uniform, vertical pencil pleats. There are three positions for the hooks. The top-most pocket is used when the curtains are suspended from a rod by means of rings, so that the rings are exposed. This position is also used when a curtain is behind a valance or pelmet. The central and bottom positions are used when the curtains are hung from a track and the curtain heading is meant to cover the track.

The gathering width for pencil pleats is two and a quarter to two and a half times the length of the track.

> **HINT** *A stunning effect is created when a second row of pencil pleat tape is sewn on just beneath the first row. When the fabric is gathered, a long, formal heading is formed that is most attractive. Be sure to line up the second row of heading tape with the first before sewing it on.*
>
>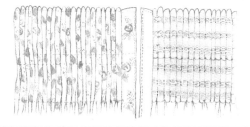

Pinch pleats

Evenly spaced pinch pleats are formed by special curtain hooks made of either metal or plastic, which are inserted into deep pockets in the heading tape. This is the most elegant and formal of the headings and is ideal for full-length and interlined curtains because the sturdy hooks and the strong cotton tape can support their weight.

The length of the neck of the metal curtain hooks varies. A long-necked hook is used for curtains which hang on rings from a rod, and medium- and short-necked hooks for curtains that hang from a track. Adjustable plastic hooks are also available. These have the advantage of not rusting and of having five optional positions. Curtains frequently 'drop',

and it is simpler to adjust the hooks than shorten the curtain!

The gathering width of the heading tape is two and a quarter to two and a half times the length of the track.

Professional curtain-makers make pinch pleats – traditionally called French pleats – by hand. This time-consuming and therefore expensive method is falling into disuse since the effect achieved by commercial tapes and hooks is similar.

Below are a few ideas for curtain headings which do not use commercial tapes or hooks.

Machine-stitched casing

An interesting effect can be achieved by forming a casing through which a curtain rod can be inserted. Fold over the top of the fabric and stitch two rows right across, 7 cm apart and 7 cm below the fold. (This size is correct for a standard wooden rod. Adjust the size of the casing to the diameter of the rod you are using. The casing should fit fairly snugly around the rod.) When the curtain rod is inserted into the casing, the fabric is gathered, resulting in an attractive frill at the top and randomly gathered pleats below, as illustrated below. This curtain is fixed and cannot be opened or closed, but it may be drawn back during the day by means of tie-backs. This method is also suitable for a valance or half-mast café-curtain. The gathering width is twice the length of the rod.

OPPOSITE: A decorative fabric border adds the finishing touch to a scalloped café-curtain with pinch pleats and loops.

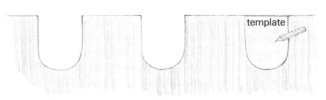

A scalloped heading with loops

This curtain heading is suitable for a half-mast café-curtain. The scallops are stitched by machine, and curtain rings are sewn onto the spaces in between. These spaces can also be extended to form loops through which a curtain rod may be inserted. The curtains are fixed and cannot be opened or closed. If the spaces are made wide enough, one or more folds may be stitched in place to create a pinch pleat effect between the scallops. The gathering width for a scalloped heading with pinch pleats is twice the length of the rod.

1. Mark scallops across the lining and fabric

2. Stitch the lining to the fabric

Both headings involve the same basic steps:

Plain scalloped heading with loops

Scalloped heading with pinch pleats

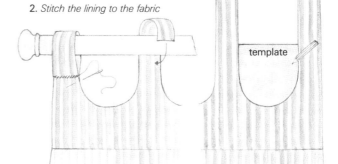

3. Make fabric loops

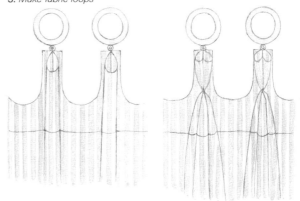

4. Alternatively, make one or two pinch pleats and sew on rings

Lining

Unless you particularly want a transparent, sheer effect, it is necessary to line curtains. The most important advantage of curtain lining is that it protects the curtain fabric from sunlight – a major consideration in very hot climates – as well as from dirt and dust. Curtains hang and drape better with the fullness that lining provides. It also improves the appearance of curtains seen from the outside as it hides the seams and joins. Lining makes curtains thicker and thus keeps out light more effectively. Lining, and particularly interlining, provides good insulation.

The lining, which is made only a little narrower than the curtains, is stitched to the top of the curtain fabric together with the heading tape.

Neat hand-made thread chains, about 2 cm in length, attach the curtain fabric to the lining at the sides of the curtain. This ensures that both the curtain and the lining can drop without interfering with the smooth flow of the curtain. When the curtains are washed, the thread chains also allow for uneven shrinkage between the curtain fabric and that of the lining.

Types of lining

Cotton lining Most textile shops sell a light-weight 100% cotton lining in white or cream. This lining is ideal as it has the same natural appearance as the curtain fabric. Because it is made of cotton, it will respond in the same way as the curtain fabric when it is washed or dry-cleaned. A further advantage is that cotton lining is available in the same width as the curtain fabric.

Cotton sateen lining If a thicker lining is required, a cotton sateen lining may be considered.

Interlining has a fluffy appearance, rather like blanketing, and is stitched in place between the curtain and lining fabrics.

This adds to the luxurious, rich, heavy appearance of the curtains, giving them extra body and therefore excellent insulation.

Block-out lining Sometimes it is desirable to cut out light altogether, for example in a nursery or a sick-room which must be kept dark during the day, bedrooms of light sleepers who are disturbed by early morning sunlight, or when street-lights are troublesome. Block-out lining, which has a specially treated rubber finish, is available for this purpose. The lining should be made separately on its own heading tape and then attached to the curtain heading tape by means of hooks, as illustrated below. The advantage of this method is that the lining can be removed when the curtains have to be cleaned. Here the gathering width of the lining doesn't have to be as full as that of the curtains and, therefore, less of this expensive lining will be needed.

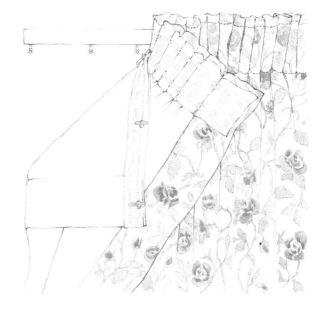

Measuring up curtains

Now that we have discussed the visual effects of curtains, the placing of curtain tracks or rods, and the choice of curtain headings, the time has come for measuring up. Once this has been done, the amount of fabric you will need may be calculated.

It is important to have the curtain track or rod in position before taking measurements.

Measure the width and the length of curtains according to the instructions for either tracks or rods.

The width

Using a metal tape measure, measure the length of the curtain track or rod (in the latter case, the distance between the two outer rings). Remember to add to your calculations any return to the ends of the track, or any overlap of the curtains in the centre. This measurement will be referred to as the *finished width*.

The length (or drop)

For the finished length measure from the top of the *curtain track* (or if using a *curtain rod*, measure from the point of suspension, that is, from the eye on the wooden ring) to the point where the completed curtain will hang, for example to the windowsill, just below the sill, or down to the floor.

Add 20-25 cm to this measurement for hem allowances and for folding over at the curtain heading. This measurement will be referred to as the *working drop*.

NOTE *The examples given are for a curtain measuring 260 cm wide with a finished length of 210 cm (the working drop = 235 cm [210 cm + 25 cm]) and gathered on a pinch pleat heading tape.*

Calculating the amount of fabric needed

FABRICS WITHOUT PATTERN REPEAT (SMALL GEOMETRIC DESIGNS)

1. *Multiply the finished width by the gathering width of the curtain heading you have chosen (e.g. 260 cm × 2.25 = 585 cm).*

2. *Divide the answer by the width of the fabric (for example 150 cm). Round up the answer to the nearest full figure in order to calculate the number of fabric widths (e.g. 585 ÷ 150 = 3.9 [4]).*

3. *Multiply the number of fabric widths by the working drop in order to calculate the amount of fabric required (e.g. 4 × 235 cm = 9.4 m).*

FABRICS WITH PATTERN REPEAT (LARGE FLORAL DESIGNS)

1. Multiply the total finished width by the gathering width of the curtain heading you have chosen (e.g. 260 cm × 2.25 = 585 cm).

2. Divide the answer by the width of the fabric (for example 150 cm). Round up the answer to the nearest full figure in order to calculate the number of fabric widths (e.g. 585 ÷ 150 = 3.9 [4]).

3. Find the pattern repeat by measuring the distance between two repeating designs, for example, pink flowers (usually 32-64 cm). Often the pattern repeat is indicated on the selvedge of the fabric (e.g. 32 cm).

4. Divide the working drop by the length of the pattern repeat and round up the answer to the next full figure (e.g. 235 cm ÷ 32 cm = 7.35 [8]).

5. Multiply this figure by the length of the pattern repeat in order to calculate the new working drop (e.g. 8 cm × 32 cm = 256).

6. In order to calculate the total amount of fabric required, multiply this new working drop by the number of fabric widths (256 cm × 4 = 10.24 m).

The rosebud design on the curtains is small and no pattern repeat is indicated *(above)*, while pattern repeat has to be taken into account when calculating fabric with the Kashmir design *(right)*.

CHAPTER THREE

FINISHING TOUCHES

It is often the finishing touches, the attention to detail that transforms the ordinary into something special. The ideas that follow offer an opportunity to be creative and individualistic.

Pelmets, valances, swags and tails, tie-backs, rosettes and bows are all accessories that often add a touch of elegance to curtains which would otherwise be very ordinary, and can dramatically affect the style of the window-dressing. They can also be instrumental in visually altering and improving the proportions of the window.

Pelmets

A pelmet is a rigid, angular construction made of board or wood and upholstered with fabric. It is fitted over the curtain track and attached to the wall by means of brackets, thereby hiding both the unsightly track and the brackets. The bottom of the pelmet may be shaped in a variety of ways. Pelmets in traditional designs lend a formal touch to a room and are suitable for an elegant lounge, dining-room or study. The pelmet may be upholstered in the same fabric as the curtain, or in a contrasting complementary design or colour. In the latter case, the fabric on the pelmet could be repeated in the tie-backs.

LEFT: Short frills outline the shape of the first three pelmets, while the fourth shows a handkerchief corner.
ABOVE: An interesting combination of a pelmet and a valance adorns the top of this window.

Valances

A valance may be described as a very short curtain, hanging from the front rail of a double track, or mounted on a wooden topboard which is hung above and in front of the curtains. In contrast to a pelmet, which is sophisticated, elegant and a bit formal, a valance is soft and informal. It is gathered on any of the curtain headings already discussed. Be generous with the amount of fabric to be gathered as the valance should be full. The depth of the curtain heading must be in proportion to the length of the valance which, in turn, should be in proportion to the length of the curtain. A general rule is that the valance is $\frac{1}{6}$ of the length of the curtain, but should never be shorter than 20 cm.

A valance may be made from the same fabric as the curtains, or in contrast to the curtains, provided the same contrast is repeated elsewhere in the room.

Frills or border patterns may be added to the bottom of the valance, or the valance may be shaped so that the sides are longer than the centre. A valance of broad broderie anglaise lace hung over a plain colour curtain looks lovely. An interesting and easy valance may be made by stitching a casing in the fabric through which the curtain rod can be inserted. In the case of a mock curtain – which is merely decorative and cannot be opened or closed – the curtain and valance may be stitched onto the same heading tape and hung from a single track or rod. A mock festoon valance with draped curves and a frill and bows is both extravagant and romantic for a girl's room.

Valances do not need to be lined since they hang in front of the curtains and are therefore protected against sunlight. However, a valance that has been lined will have more body and will hang better.

A valance may be used to cover an ugly, old-fashioned wooden pelmet. This is done by gathering the valance on a heading tape in the normal way and then nailed to the pelmet with upholstery tacks. Screw eyes may also be inserted all the way around the pelmet, and the curtain hooks on the heading tape hooked into these, as illustrated below.

When using a double track, the valance must be folded around the ends of the front track towards the back so that the outer two hooks can be attached to the outer two screw eyes on the back track.

Examples of a variety of valances are illustrated below.

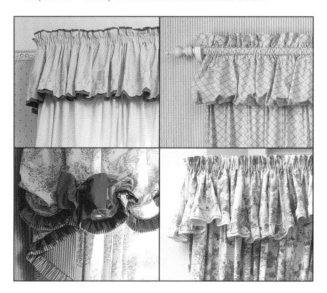

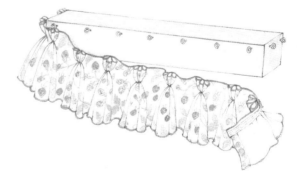

A border of contrasting green outlines the shape of these stunning cream swags and tails and is repeated down the insides of the curtains.

Swags and tails

This may be best described as a pelmet consisting of one or more draped, pleated swags with tails which hang down the sides in graceful curves. The effect is dramatic, formal and elegant – almost theatrical – and will turn a plain window, which would otherwise be insignificant, into a focal point. Swags and tails may be used successfully with curtains or Roman blinds, or they may be the only decoration for a window where the effect is more important than the practical considerations.

The swag is usually cut on the bias, which helps it to drape naturally into folds, and is lined with cotton lining. Tails are cut separately and are usually lined with fabric in a plain colour or contrasting design in order to emphasize the folds. These different sections are mounted on a wooden topboard which has been positioned, using angle brackets, on the wall above the curtains.

Making a single swag and one pair of tails

Although the finished tails appear to be natural extensions of the swag, they are made separately. All the sections are then attached to a topboard which is fitted over the window.

MEASURING

To calculate the width, decide how far the topboard is to extend beyond the window. If it is to fit over a curtain track, allow a few centimetres extra. This is the finished width of the swag and tails.

To calculate the length of the swag, measure the length of the window and take one sixth to one eighth of this measurement as the finished length of the swag at its deepest point.

The length of the tails is a matter of preference but a general guideline is that the tails should hang about a third to half-way down the length of the window. (The short vertical side of the tail is a fifth to an eighth of this length.)

REQUIREMENTS

❏ *Fabric for the swag:* Using the finished width and length of the swag, make a template according to the proportions shown *(Fig. 1)*. Allow enough fabric for the template to be positioned diagonally over the fabric so that it can be cut on the bias.

❏ *For the tails:* Make a template using the finished length of the tails as well as the length of the short side and calculating the cut width as follows: (the number of folds [usually three to four] x 2 x width of the fold) + 1 width of the fold + 1 width of the return of the topboard *(Fig. 2)*. If the fabric for the tails has a one-way pattern, a length of fabric twice the length of

the template will be required. With a plain fabric, you may only need one length, depending on the width of the template. When cutting out the fabric for the left tail, place the template face down on the fabric.

❏ *For the binding at the top:* Use an offcut of the fabric measuring twice the return of the topboard by the length of the top-board.

❏ *Contrasting lining:* For the swag, you will need fabric the same size as the template. For the tails, you will need enough contrasting fabric to cut out two tails to the size of the template.

❏ *Topboard:* To measure the finished width of the swag by a 12-15 cm return.

❏ *Tacks or staple gun*

❏ *Angle brackets*

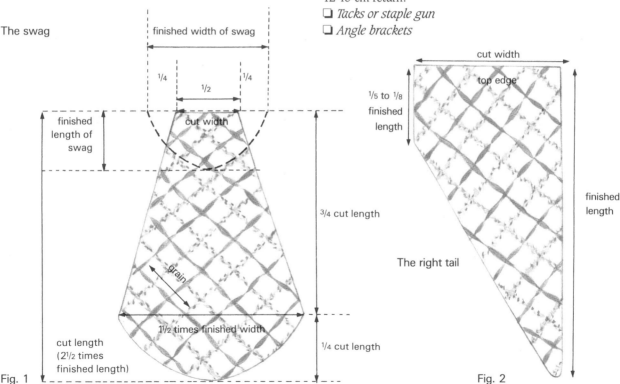

The swag

finished width of swag

¹/₄   ¹/₂   ¹/₄

cut width

finished length of swag

cut width

³/₄ cut length

grain

1¹/₂ times finished width

¹/₄ cut length

cut length (2¹/₂ times finished length)

Fig. 1

cut width

top edge

¹/₅ to ¹/₈ finished length

finished length

The right tail

Fig. 2

METHOD

Swag

1. With right sides together, join the fabric and lining by stitching round three sides and leaving the top open for turning through (Fig. 3).

2. Turn through, press seams and secure top edge with tacking stitches.

3. Mark the centre and the finished width of the swag on the work surface and then, working inwards from the outer edge, fold up one long side of the fabric into pleats (three to four pleats, each measuring about 8-10 cm, is a rough guide). Do the same on the other side so that the inside pleats are an equal distance from the centre. When all the pleats have been folded and pinned, the top should measure the finished width of the swag. Machine stitch across the top to secure all the folds (Fig. 4).

4. With right sides together, sew the binding strip over this line of stitching, fold the binding over and slipstitch it to the underside, covering all raw edges (Fig. 5).

Tails

1. With right sides together, join fabric and lining of the right tail by stitching along all sides except at the top (Fig. 6).

2. Turn through, press seams and secure the top edge with tacking stitches.

3. Fold in pleats from the short side to the back to the required width, leaving a piece to fold around the return of the topboard (Fig. 7 & 8).

4. Bind the top edge as for the swag (Fig. 9).

5. Repeat this process for the left tail.

Fig. 6   Fig. 7   Fig. 8   Fig. 9

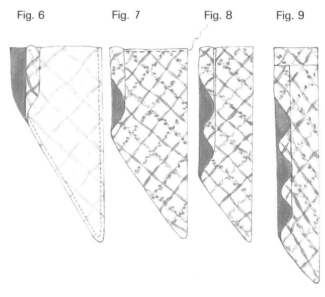

centre

Fig. 3   Fig. 4

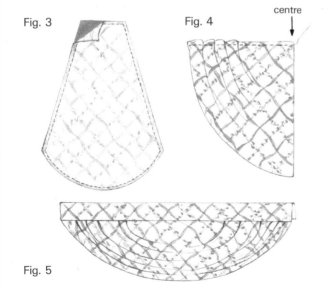

Fig. 5

HINT Make templates for swags and tails according to your specific measurements and take them along to the shop and position them on the fabric to ensure that you purchase the correct amount of fabric.

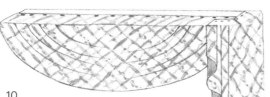

Fig. 10

TO COMPLETE

1. *Tack or staple the different sections to the topboard. The tails may be positioned over or under the swag, with the unfolded part covering the return of the topboard (Fig. 10).*

2. *Mount the topboard to the wall or window frame with angle brackets.*

BELOW: A beautiful 'over the top' arrangement of swags and tails with bow rosettes dress up this tiny window.
RIGHT: The fabric of the swag is repeated in the lining of the tail.

Different lengths of plain pink fabric have been artistically draped over a brass curtain rod to stunning effect.

Draping fabric over curtain rods

A stunning effect may be achieved by simply draping a length or two of fabric over a curtain rod. This method of dressing a window is more informal and less structured than swags and tails, and less complicated to put together. It is an ideal way of focusing attention on a window and highlighting its significance in the overall decorating scheme of a room.

Where privacy is not important, loose drapes may be used as the only decoration of a window (these are obviously not functional), or they may be used together with curtains or blinds. If used with curtains, the track for the curtains should be positioned behind the rod over which the fabric is to be draped. Enough space should be allowed between the track and the rod to ensure that the movement of the curtains is not obstructed. The rod should extend sufficiently beyond the edges of the window, and the end finials should be particularly attractive.

A wide variety of effects are possible with draping, none of them difficult. For a simple symmetrical effect, a single length of fabric can be draped over a rod to form one loose, deep swag with a tail down either side ending in a 'pool' of fabric on the floor. The fabric requirement here will be twice the length to the floor, plus the amount which rests on the floor, plus one and a half times the length of the rod.

If the fabric is to be wound several times around the rod to produce more swags, the amount of fabric must be increased accordingly.

In the case of an unlined piece of fabric, the sides must be hemmed, or they may be trimmed with a contrasting binding or border – this will create an interesting effect as the fabric snakes around the rod.

Alternatively, the fabric may be lined with a contrasting design or colour, and draped in such a way as to show up the contrast effectively. If the ends of the fabric are cut diagonally, this will result in a tailed effect down the sides once the fabric is hung.

Tie-backs

The practical advantages of tie-backs are that they can be used to tie back curtains during the day in order to admit light, as well as to allow easy access through glass sliding doors. But even more important is their aesthetic value. Tie-backs provide that ultimate finishing touch which can transform the merely ordinary into something special. The attractive draped effect of curtains which have been tied back will also help to soften the angular lines of a window. In addition, different effects may be achieved, depending on the height at which the tie-backs are applied. Usually tie-backs are positioned two-thirds down the length of the curtains. Their position may also be influenced by other factors, for example, when the curtains are used together with a blind or when there is a windowsill. In such cases, the tie-backs are lined up with the windowsill.

Tie-backs may be made in the same fabric as the curtains and piped with a contrasting plain colour or they can be made using a contrasting design or colour which is present elsewhere in the room, thereby linking them up with the total decorating theme.

Making shaped tie-backs

MEASURING

To determine the length of each tie-back, use a tape measure to tie back the curtains to achieve the required effect. The reading on the tape measure will be the finished length of each tie-back (see *Hint* opposite).

REQUIREMENTS
❏ *Fabric:* Enough for four pattern pieces (see *Hint* opposite).
❏ *Interlining:* Enough for two pattern pieces.
❏ *Piping:* To go round both tie-backs.
❏ *Four plastic curtain rings:* These rings are sewn onto each end of each tie-back and hooked onto cup hooks inserted in the wall.

A plain piped and shaped tie-back *(top left)* looks smart on its own but can be adorned with a choux rosette *(top right)*, a folded bow *(bottom left)* or a double bow rosette *(bottom right)*.

HINT *This is a useful guide to the sizes of tie-backs in relation to the size of the curtain and the amount of fabric to be purchased.*

Number of drops per curtain	Length of one tie-back	Fabric for two tie-backs
1 drop (150 cm)	55-60 cm	40 cm
2 drops (300 cm)	75-80 cm	50 cm
3 drops (450 cm)	85-100 cm	80 cm
4 drops (600 cm)	120-140 cm	1 m

METHOD

1. *Make a template by drawing the desired shape and size on folded paper (so that the two halves will be identical). Add a seam allowance of 1,5 cm right round and cut out the template* (Fig. 11).

2. *Cut out four pieces of fabric, using the template as a pattern* (Fig. 12).

3. *Cut out two pieces of interlining, using the template as a pattern* (Fig. 13).

4. *Tack one interlining to the wrong side of one of the pieces of fabric* (Fig. 14).

5. *Tack the piping to the right side of the fabric, keeping raw edges together. Join the ends of the piping neatly together by inserting one raw edge inside the other and stitching* (Fig. 15).

6. *With right sides together, position a second piece of fabric over the first, tack and stitch, using the zipper foot, right round, leaving a small opening for turning through* (Fig. 16).

7. *Turn through and slipstitch the opening closed* (Fig. 17). *Press.*

8. *Sew a plastic ring onto each end of the tie-back* (Fig. 17).

9. *Repeat steps 4-8 for the second tie-back.*

Different options for the shape of the tie-back

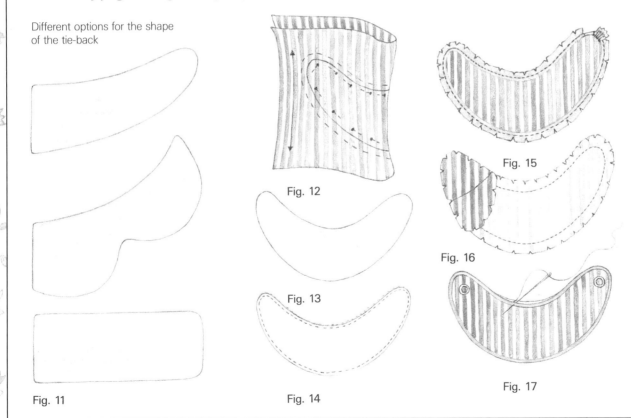

Fig. 11

Fig. 12

Fig. 13

Fig. 14

Fig. 15

Fig. 16

Fig. 17

The three designs used to make the plaited tie-back echo the colour scheme throughout the room.

Making plaited tie-backs

MEASURING
Determine the finished length of the tie-backs as before.

REQUIREMENTS
❏ *Fabric* – about 20-25 cm of three different colours to make two tubes in each colour.
❏ *Interlining* – enough for six tubes, about 75 cm.
❏ *Four plastic rings*

METHOD
1. *Tack the interlining onto the wrong side of each strip of fabric.*
2. *With right sides together, fold each strip in half lengthwise and stitch along the long edge, then turn through (Fig. 18 & 19).*

3. *Position the seam in the centre on the underside of each tube, fold over both ends of each tube and stitch to secure (Fig. 20).*
4. *Slipstitch the ends of three different coloured tubes together and plait. Slipstitch the ends together when plaiting is complete (Fig. 21).*
5. *Sew the plastic rings onto each end of each plaited tie-back (Fig. 22).*

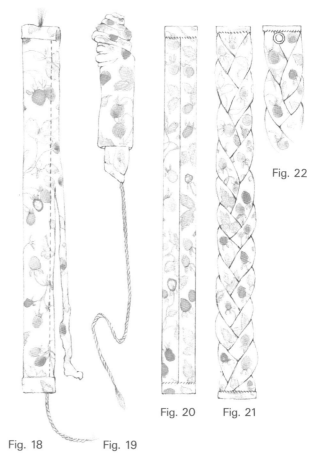

Fig. 22

Fig. 18   Fig. 19   Fig. 20   Fig. 21

Bows and rosettes

Bows and rosettes are used to focus attention on certain areas of the window-dressing. They add interesting final touches to swags and tails, blinds, valances and tie-backs.

Piped bow

The pieces for this bow are interlined and piped *(see tie-backs, p. 48)*.

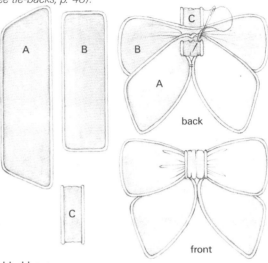

Choux rosette

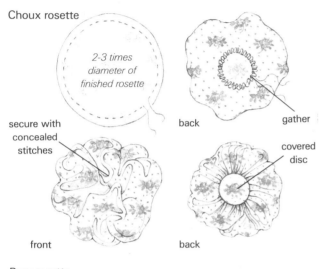

2-3 times diameter of finished rosette

secure with concealed stitches

back

gather

front

back

covered disc

Bow rosette

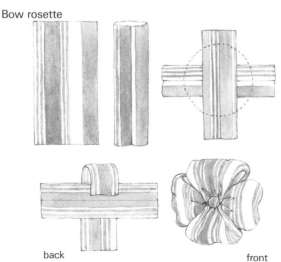

back

front

Folded bow

The pieces of the folded bow are hemmed right round.

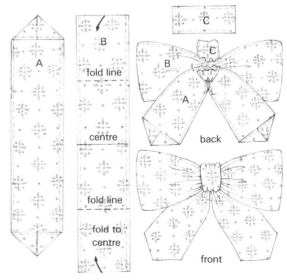

fold line

centre

fold line

fold to centre

back

front

Edgings

Frills and prairie points are decorative edgings and finish off curtains, valances, blinds and tie-backs beautifully.

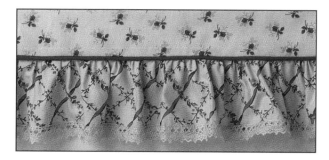

Single frill with lace edging

Two single frills gathered together

Contrasting fabric of back frill edges pleated front frill

Prairie points

width 14 cm

length 14 cm

1. *Cut out enough squares in different colours and designs to make up the length required. Fold each piece into a small square.*

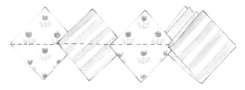

2. *Line up the small folded squares so that they overlap slightly, and stitch through centre.*

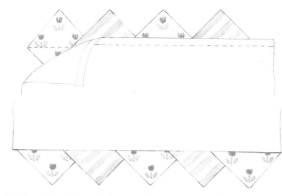

3. *Position right side of fabric over strip of squares and sew just under previous stitching line on strip. Fold right side of fabric up and iron flat. (Prairie points have been used to edge the curtains on p. 60.)*

CHAPTER FOUR

BLINDS

Blinds offer infinite scope as an alternative way to decorate windows. They are practical and functional and draw away to expose much of the window. They are easily incorporated into the overall decorating scheme of a room, and are often the solution to decorating 'difficult' windows.

Blinds differ from curtains in that they are raised by means of a roller or cord system, whereas curtains must be drawn sideways to expose the window.

Roller blinds

These simple, neat and practical blinds date back to the Georgian and Victorian eras, when they were in common use. The rectangular piece of stiffened fabric draws down from a roller fitted into special brackets. A spring mechanism on one side controls and fixes the position to which the blind is drawn. The fabric rolls up neatly around the wooden roller to form a cylinder that sits unobtrusively at the top of the window. Roller blinds can be fitted inside the reveal or on the outside of the window. On their own, roller blinds are rather austere and are often used for precisely this reason – to create a minimal effect. In kitchens and bathrooms where an uncluttered effect is often required and where heat and steam may be a problem, these blinds are a good choice. They offer a practical solution where space is limited above a window or when a window opens to the inside of a room.

Roller blinds can be teamed with a pelmet, valance or swag and tails – under which they will disappear when rolled up – to soften the effect. Mock curtains can be added to this arrangement to create a more formal effect. In this case, the roller blind will serve as the functional part - covering the window when needed and disappearing behind the pelmet or valance when rolled up.

An ideal way of finishing a roller blind is to use a co-ordinating border pattern to decorate the bottom edge.

Roller blinds are best left to the specialists to make because the stiffening and bonding of the fabric is a rather tricky operation requiring specialist equipment. If you do have access to a business that will commercially stiffen or bond your fabric for you, you can make a roller blind yourself. The rest of the materials needed can be bought in kit form with the manufacturer's instructions included.

The bottom of a roller blind can be finished with a variety of scalloped edges and rounded off with bias binding. A pretty, coordinating fabric border sewn on just above the scallop adds a finishing touch.

Roman blinds

These blinds are neatly tailored and have an elegant simplicity. When the blind is down, it looks like a rectangular, flat piece of fabric. The blind is pulled up into symmetrical concertina pleats by means of the cord system at the back. Because the blind folds away so trimly, it admits the maximum amount of light.

A Roman blind is a good choice when the window-dressing needs to be understated so that the architectural features of a window may be displayed. An example here would be a beautiful sash window with wooden frames and architrave, and in this case the blind would be mounted inside the reveal. These blinds are suitable in a room where a simple, linear approach has been used for the interior decoration. They are a practical option for windows requiring a limited volume of fabric, for example above the basin or washing surface in a kitchen or bathroom, for a window above a desk or in a 'busy' area such as a playroom.

In order to round off the blinds with a little more detail, edgings may be used. These can be in a contrasting plain colour or in one of the great variety of interesting border patterns that are available. The edging may be applied right around the blind or only along the bottom edge.

If the angularity of these blinds is too stark for your taste, a softer, more feminine effect may be achieved by adding a small pleated frill made from fabric or anglaise lace to the bottom of the blind. The bottom edge may also be scalloped and edged with a contrasting binding.

It is preferable to line Roman blinds with cotton lining as this protects the fabric against sunlight, allows the blind to hang better, provides good insulation, keeps out light, and disguises the 'mechanics' of the cord system at the back.

Many of the modern fabric designs are suitable for Roman blinds and I prefer not to be too directive in this respect. Traditionally, striped and geometric designs are suitable because they conform to the linear simplicity of the blinds.

A fabric border frames this Roman blind which is in turn framed by the wooden architrave of a sash window.

If floral designs are more appropriate to the materials in the rest of the room, edgings may be used to emphasize the geometric shape of the blind, thereby framing the flowers, as it were.

Roman blinds are very successful in their own right, but they may also be used with curtains or mock curtains. In the case of mock curtains, these are used together with the blind to create a draped effect in the room, and serve a purely decorative function. If additional decoration is required above the window, swags and tails may be used very favourably with Roman blinds.

The blind may be mounted in the reveal or over the window frame. If used with curtains, it must be mounted inside the reveal. By positioning the blind over the window frame, you can cover up a window with irregular proportions, as found particularly in older houses, or create the illusion of a larger window. In order to admit as much light as possible, the blind may be mounted a little distance above the window so that most of the window is exposed when the blind is raised. A Roman blind is about 25-30 cm deep when folded into a completely raised position.

Making a Roman blind

There are various methods for making up a Roman blind. Each of them is based on approximately the same principles, and the blinds are raised and lowered by means of a cord system at the back. The method described below is, in my opinion, the neatest, since only single rows of horizontal stitching show at the front.

MEASURING

If the blind is to fit inside the window reveal, measure the width and the height of the window. The size of the completed blind will be 1 cm less than these measurements. If you wish to mount the blind on the wall above the window, decide how far it should extend on all sides, and measure accordingly – this will be the size of the completed blind.

PLANNING THE NUMBER OF FOLDS IN THE RAISED BLIND

The distance between the casings (in which the dowel rods will be inserted) will determine the depth of the folds. This distance will be subject to the length of the blind, but 24-34 cm will be appropriate in most cases. The folds formed when raising the blind will then be between 12-17 cm.

If a decorative border is to be added to the bottom of the blind, this must be displayed even when the blind is raised. The distance from the top of this border to the first casing should be half the distance between that of the following casings. The distance between the last casing and the top of the blind must be larger (about one and a half times). These extra centimetres allow the folds to lie neatly on top of one another when the blind is fully raised, and also provide space for the casings and rings which accumulate at the top.

Fig. 1

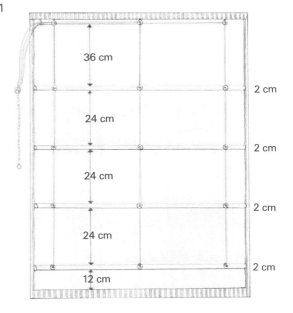

36 cm

2 cm

24 cm

2 cm

24 cm

2 cm

24 cm

2 cm

12 cm

The measurements given are examples only

REQUIREMENTS

❏ *Fabric for the blind:* Take the measurement of the completed blind and add 10 cm to the width and 20 cm to the length measurements to obtain the final cutting width and length. In order to establish the number of drops required, the final cutting width is divided by the width of the fabric (e.g., 150 cm). Multiply the number of drops by the final cutting length, and this is the quantity of fabric required.

HINTS *If the window to be covered is very wide, more than one blind is preferable. However, if the fabric has to be joined, it is better to obtain the desired width by stitching equal sections of fabric from the second drop onto both sides of the first drop. A decorative border pattern may be applied over these joins.*
☆ *If the width of the blind is just a fraction more than the width of the fabric (e.g., 165 cm), a border pattern may be added to both sides in order to gain the extra width required.*

❏ *Lining fabric (use any 100% cotton lining):* The total width of the lining is the same as for the fabric. For the length, add on 2 cm per casing to the final length measurement of the fabric. Calculate the amount of lining required in exactly the same way as for the fabric, using the above final width and length measurements.

❏ *A wooden lath:* The top end of the blind is mounted on a wooden lath measuring 2 cm thick and 5 cm wide with a length equal to the width of the completed blind.

❏ *A flat wooden batten:* This serves as a weight at the bottom of the blind – about 1 cm thick and 5 cm wide. It should be about 10 cm shorter than the width of the blind.

❏ *Left-over lining:* A small piece to cover the wooden batten and the wooden lath.

❏ *Dowel rods.*

❏ *Plastic rings:* Allow three to four per casing.

❏ *Velcro:* The width of the completed blind.

❏ *Nylon cord.*

The bold vertical stripes on the fabric complement the linear simplicity of this Roman blind, which is teamed with curtains in a pretty floral design.

❏ *Screw eyes:* Size No. 9, brass-plated screw eyes for screwing into the lath and through which the cords on the blind will be threaded. The number is the same as the number of rings on one casing, plus one extra.

❏ *A brass or plastic cleat:* Mount the cleat at a convenient position on either the wall or the window frame. The nylon cord is secured to this once the blind is raised.

METHOD

1. *Press in 6 cm to the wrong side on either side of the lining.*

2. *Starting at the bottom of the blind, measure the distance for the first casing stitching line. (This will be the distance between the casings divided by 2. For example, if the distance between the casings is 24 cm, mark the first casing stitching line at 12 cm. Mark the second stitching line at 14 cm. The casing stitching lines must be 2 cm apart to accommodate the dowel rods [Fig. 1, p. 56].)*

3. *Continue measuring and marking the rest of the casing stitching lines along the length of the fabric, making them the full distance apart (e.g. 24 cm) and 2 cm wide. Remember to make the distance between the last casing stitching line and the top of the blind further apart than the rest (e.g. 36 cm) in order to accommodate the folds, casings and rings as mentioned previously (Fig. 1, p. 56).*

4. *Cut a left-over piece of lining which will comfortably accommodate the wooden batten when folded double (wrong sides together) and pressed in at the sides. With wrong sides together, fold the lining for the blind so that the first two casing stitching lines line up, slip in the casing for the wooden batten and stitch the raw edges of the batten casing together with the first casing of the lining. The casing for the dowel rod must be on the right side of the lining for the blind, and the casing for the wooden batten must be on the wrong side (Fig. 2 & 3).*

5. *Stitch the next set of marked lines to form further casings of 1 cm each, again on the right side (outside) of the lining.*

6. *Press in 5 cm on each side of the fabric for the blind.*

7. *With right sides together, stitch the lining onto the fabric along the bottom edge (Fig. 4).*

8. *Turn out and make a 10 cm fold at the bottom of the fabric (so that the lining only begins 10 cm from the bottom) (Fig. 5).*

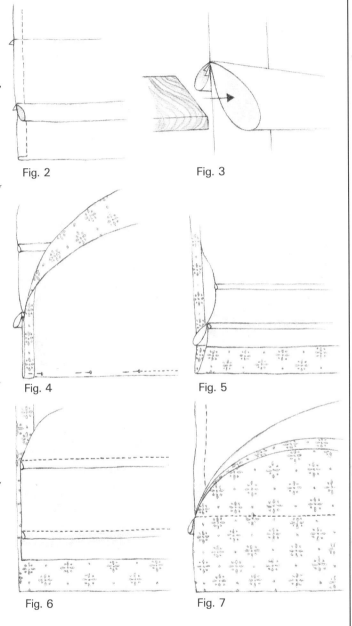

Fig. 2

Fig. 3

Fig. 4

Fig. 5

Fig. 6

Fig. 7

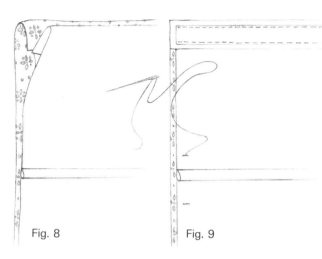

Fig. 8

Fig. 9

9. *Pin and tack the fabric and lining together, making sure that they are smoothly and evenly lined up* (Fig. 6). *Stitch the lining and fabric together along the casing stitching lines, taking care not to stitch through the casings* (Fig. 7).

10. *Measure the blind from top to bottom and mark the fabric so that it measures 2 cm more than the required completed length of the blind. Cut off the excess fabric at the top. Fold the 2 cm under (fabric and lining) to the wrong side and press flat* (Fig. 8).

11. *Stitch one of the strips of Velcro tape on the lining side, right at the top of the blind* (Fig. 9).

12. *Catch the lining to the fabric with a small stitch 4 cm either side of each casing (on the inside of the blind) to prevent the lining from gaping* (Fig. 9).

13. *Insert the wooden batten into the hidden lining casing, and the dowel rods into the other casings.*

14. *Sew on the rings at equal intervals across the width of the casings, the two outer rings being 8 cm from the edges of the blind. Make sure that the rings are in identical positions relative to one another on all the casings* (Fig. 1, p. 56).

15. *Cover the wooden lath with a piece of offcut fabric or lining and staple (or glue) the reciprocal strip of Velcro to the front* (Fig. 10).

16. *Taking the Velcro strip as the front, screw in the screw eyes on the underside of the lath exactly in line with the rings on the blind. Screw in one additional eye on the side which will take the draw-cord* (Fig. 11).

17. *Press the Velcro strip on the blind onto the one attached to the lath.*

18. *Thread the nylon cord through the rings from bottom to top, and then through the screw eyes and to the side where the draw-cord will be. Now knot the cords to the bottom row of rings* (Fig. 1, p. 56).

19. *Knot all the cords together at the point where they come through the extra screw eye. Trim the cords to the same length where they can be reached when the blind is down. Plait the cords to form a single draw-cord* (Fig. 1, p. 56).

20. *Detach the Velcro strips from one another, and mount the wooden lath on the wall or in the window reveal by means of screws. Re-attach the two Velcro strips.*

21. *Attach a cleat to the wall on the side of the draw-cord so that the cord can be wound around this when the blind is raised.*

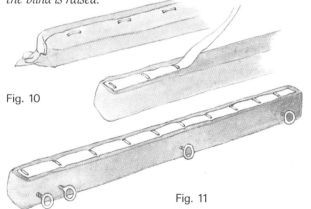

Fig. 10

Fig. 11

A controversy exists about the terminology for two of the ruched blinds. To avoid confusion, in this book, the festoon blind is understood as being the one which hangs out smoothly when lowered, and an Austrian blind as the one that is permanently ruched along its length even when it is lowered.

Festoon blinds

Like the Roman blind, a festoon blind is raised by means of a cord system, but because the fabric of the blind is gathered in the width as well – usually twice the width of the window – the effect is dramatically different from that of a Roman blind. When the blind is lowered, it looks almost like a curtain, except for the soft drapes at the bottom which hang across the window width in equally spaced curves. When the blind is raised, these curves become fuller, creating a graceful, rounded effect. The gentle line of the curves is usually emphasized by means of a gathered frill added to the bottom of the blind. A really luxurious impression can be created by adding these gathered frills to the sides of the blind as well. At the top, the width of the fabric is gathered on a heading tape which forms pencil pleats.

Because these blinds are so decorative, they can be an asset in many interior decorating schemes. They are very suited to a room where the décor is lavish and extravagant, but they may also be used as an interesting contrast in an otherwise understated interior. These blinds are an excellent choice for windows with beautiful wooden architraves and classic proportions as they draw attention to these features. Festoon blinds make an uninteresting window more lively (for example, in a bathroom or guest toilet), and with the addition of a few matching accessories, this is often all the decoration that is needed.

A great advantage of these blinds is that they look so effective when raised – a feature which is not shared by some other blinds and curtains. But bear in mind that their mini-

A frilled festoon blind covers this window while curtains edged in prairie points hang in front.

mum length, when raised, is about 50 cm. They should be mounted, therefore, a fair distance above windows where a maximum amount of light is needed.

Medium-weight fabrics are very suitable for festoon blinds as they drape and fold beautifully. Here, too, there are few restrictions in the type of pattern you can choose. Floral designs are by their very nature suited to the feminine character of the blinds, but stripes, used either vertically or horizontally, can be very effective.

As already mentioned, a gathered or pleated frill is usually added onto the bottom of the blind. The frill may be made in the same fabric as the main blind, or in a contrasting design or colour. Alternatively, broderie anglaise lace or a pretty cotton lace can also be used, while narrow piping, in a plain colour and surrounding the blind on all sides, adds just that little touch of elegance and finish.

Mount festoon blinds either in the window reveal or on the wall above the window. The latter is a good option if the illusion of a larger window is desired, or when an unattractive or irregular window needs to be disguised.

Provided they are not exposed to direct sunlight, these blinds may remain unlined. Unlined blinds have a hazy, translucent effect on the light which filters through from behind, creating a harmony of light and shadow with the folds of the drapes.

Where protection against sunlight is necessary and where light entering the room must be limited, the blinds can be backed with a cotton lining which has the same qualities as the fabric in terms of 'dropping' and shrinkage during washing.

Making a festoon blind

MEASURING

Measure the window reveal in order to establish the length and the width of the blind. Take 1 cm off both measurements. This will be the size of the finished blind.

If the blind is to be fitted over the window, add on the preferred distance it should extend beyond the length and width of the window. This will be the size of the finished blind.

REQUIREMENTS

❑ *Fabric for blind:* For the 'body' of the blind, take the pattern repeat of the fabric into account and use the relevant formula (p.37, steps 1 & 2) to establish the number of drops required. Bear in mind that the gathering width is twice the finished width of the blind. Add 30 cm to the finished length in order to determine the working drop (or cut length), and multiply this by the number of drops required. This gives you the total amount of fabric needed. The additional 30 cm is essential to give the festooned effect at the bottom of the blind when it is fully lowered.

For a single frill at the bottom of the blind, multiply the number of drops (above) by 2 to find the number of fabric strips needed, and multiply this by the depth of the frill (plus 3 cm for hem and seam allowances).

For a double frill, multiply the number of fabric strips by twice the depth of the frill plus a seam allowance.

❑ *Lining:* The lining requirement is the same as for the fabric for the 'body' of the blind.

❑ *Piping:* Take the width of the ungathered blind and add on a 2 cm seam allowance. (If piping is to go down both sides and across the top and bottom of the blind, piping measuring twice the length and twice the width will be required.)

❑ *Heading tape (for pencil pleats):* Take the width measurement of the ungathered blind and add on a 2 cm seam allowance.

❑ *Velcro tape:* Take the width measurement of the ungathered blind.

❑ *Gathering tape (narrow rufflette):* The strips are sewn along the length of the blind, the outside strips 10 cm in from the edges and thereafter spaced 60-80 cm apart. Work out the number of strips needed and multiply by the cut length.

❑ *Plastic rings:* Enough to space them 25 cm apart along each strip of gathering tape.

❑ *Wooden lath:* To mount the blind at the top, a wooden lath measuring 3 cm x 5 cm x the finished width of blind is required.

❑ *Screw eyes:* One size No. 9, brass-plated screw eye to correspond with each strip of gathering tape, plus one extra.

❑ *Nylon cord*

❑ *Cleat:* For accommodating the draw-cord.

METHOD

1. Cut out fabric drops and join after pattern matching.

2. With right sides and raw edges together, sew piping to bottom edge of fabric (as well as down the sides and across the top, if required) (Fig. 12).

3. Cut fabric strips for frill, join and gather to required width.

4. With right sides (of frill and fabric) and raw edges together, position frill over piping and stitch along previous stitching line, using the zipper foot of your machine (Fig. 13).

5. With right sides together, join fabric and lining by stitching down one side, across the bottom and up along the other side. Take care not to catch the frill at the bottom (Fig. 14).

6. Turn inside out and press seams.

7. Pin or tack vertical rows of gathering tape (narrow rufflette) along the length of the blind, 10 cm in from the sides and 60-80 cm apart. Stitch these in position from the front of the fabric (Fig. 15).

8. Sew plastic rings to the rows of tape, 12 cm from the bottom and 25 cm apart. The last of these rings must be 25 cm from the top (Fig. 16).

9. Fold the raw edges at the top to the back and press. Position the heading tape over the fold, and stitch (Fig. 16).

10. Position the Velcro tape on top of the heading tape and stitch, taking care that the stitching does not interfere with the gathering cords on the tape (Fig. 16). Gather the heading tape to the finished width of the blind.

11. Cover the wooden lath with a piece of offcut fabric or lining and staple (or glue) the reciprocal strip of Velcro to the front (Fig. 10, p. 59).

12. Taking the Velcro strip as the front, screw in the screw eyes on the underside of the lath exactly in line with the rings on the blind. Screw in one additional eye on the side which will take the draw-cord (Fig. 17).

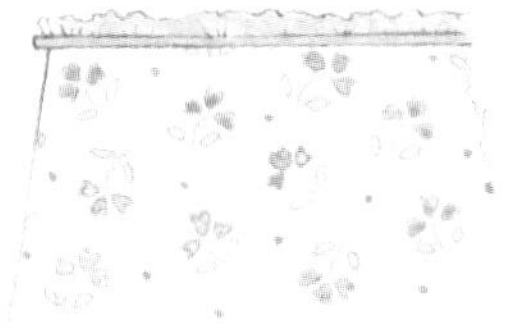

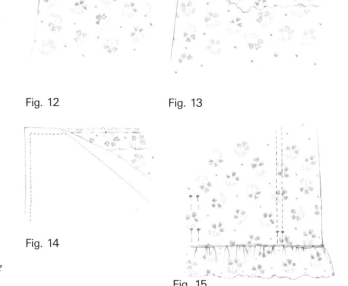

Fig. 12   Fig. 13

Fig. 14

Fig. 15

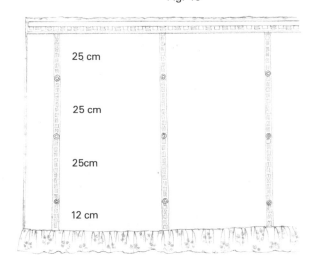

25 cm

25 cm

25cm

12 cm

Fig. 16

13. *Press the Velcro strip on the blind onto the one on the lath.*

14. *Thread the nylon cord through the rings from bottom to top, and then through the screw eyes and to the side where the draw-cord will be. Now knot the cords to the bottom row of rings (Fig. 18).*

15. *Hold all the cords together and pull them simultaneously so that the blind ruches up to the desired finished length (Fig. 18). Tie a knot at the point where the cords leave the last screw eye and secure a curtain ring to the knot (Fig. 19). The ring will catch on the screw eye when the blind is lowered, thus ensuring that the blind retains its ruched swags at the bottom.*

16. *Detach the Velcro strips from one another, and mount the wooden lath on the wall or in the window reveal by means of screws (Fig. 20). Re-attach the two Velcro strips.*

17. *Attach a cleat to the wall on the side of the draw-cord so that the cord can be wound around this when the blind is raised.*

Fig. 17

Fig. 18

HINT *An interesting effect can be achieved if the sides of the blind are not corded. This results in 'tails' on either side when the cords are drawn.*

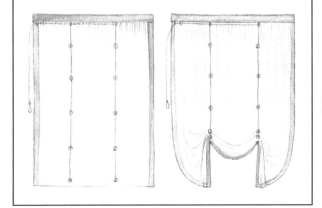

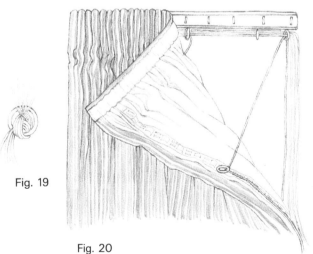

Fig. 19

Fig. 20

Austrian blinds

An Austrian blind differs from a festoon blind in that its length is gathered into equally spaced curves, resulting in drapes which are permanent even when the blind is fully down. This effect is enhanced when the blind is raised. The extra fabric (calculated at one and a half to two times the length), as well as the full, draped effect, make these blinds more extravagant and flamboyant than festoon blinds.

The decorating principles for festoon blinds also apply to Austrian blinds. They are unsuitable for tall, narrow windows as the blinds need sufficient width for at least three

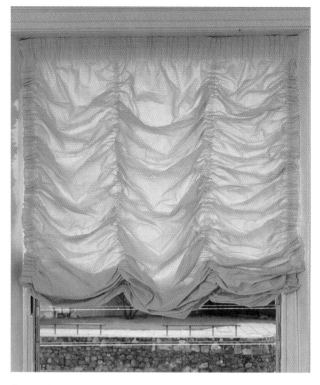

Cotton lining was used for both the front and the lining of this Austrian blind mounted within the reveal of a sash window. These charming blinds can also be made very successfully out of lace.

HINT *Festoon and Austrian blinds may also be mounted on a curtain rod.*

or four curves spaced approximately 20-30 cm apart. The bottom of the blind can be finished with a gathered fabric or lace frill although frills at the sides are not recommended. These blinds may be lined or unlined.

Large floral designs should be avoided since the effect of these blinds is already somewhat elaborate. Choose a fabric with a simple design so that the accent falls on the draped effect. An Austrian blind made from soft cotton lining with a frill of coarse lace at the bottom can look very effective.

Making an Austrian blind

MEASURING

Measure the window reveal in order to establish the length and the width of the blind. Take 1 cm off both measurements. This will be the size of the finished blind.

If the blind is to be fitted over the window, add on the preferred distance it should extend beyond the length and width of the window. This will be the size of the finished blind.

REQUIREMENTS

❏ *Fabric for blind:* For the 'body' of the blind, take the pattern repeat of the fabric into account and use the relevant formula (p.37, steps 1 & 2) to establish the number of drops required. Bear in mind that the gathering width is two to two and a half times the finished width of the blind. The working drop (cut length) is one and a half to two times the finished length of the blind. Multiply the number of drops by the length of the working drop to determine the amount of fabric.

For a single frill at the bottom, multiply the number of drops (above) by 2 to find the number of fabric strips needed. Multiply this by the depth of the frill (plus 3 cm for hem and seam allowances). For a double frill: Multiply the number of fabric strips by twice the depth of the frill plus seam allowance.

❏ *Lining:* The lining requirement is the same as for the fabric for the 'body' of the blind.

❏ *Piping:* Take the width measurement of the ungathered blind and add on a 2 cm seam allowance.

❏ *Heading tape (for pencil pleats):* Take the width measurement of the ungathered blind and add on a 2 cm turn over allowance.

❏ *Velcro tape:* Take the width measurement of the ungathered blind.

❏ *Gathering tape (narrow rufflette):* The strips are sewn along the length of the blind, the outside strips positioned 2 cm in from the edges and thereafter spaced 50-60 cm apart. Work out the number of strips required.

> **HINT** *Instead of rufflette gathering tape and rings, a special Austrian blind tape may be used. This tape has woven nylon loops through which the cord system is threaded.*

❏ *Plastic rings:* Enough to space them 25 cm apart along each strip of gathering tape.

❏ *Wooden lath:* For mounting the blind at the top – 3 cm x 5 cm x the finished width of the blind.

❏ *Screw eyes:* One size No. 9, brass-plated screw eye to correspond with each strip of gathering tape, plus one extra to accommodate all the cords.

❏ *Nylon cord*

❏ *Cleat:* For accommodating the draw-cord at the side of the window.

METHOD

Follow the instructions for making a festoon blind but position the outside strips of gathering tape 2 cm in from the edges of the blind. Before the blind is strung, draw in the vertical strips of gathering tape until the blind measures the required finished length, as illustrated below.

The following blinds are variations of their predecessors', and the same principles apply as to where and how they should be used. I am not giving detailed descriptions of their construction but the methods already described, together with explanatory illustrations, should be helpful should you wish to make them.

Pleated festoon blinds (Box blinds)

These blinds belong to the same family as festoon blinds. However, instead of gathering the width at the top of the blind by means of a heading tape, inverted box pleats are formed at regular intervals and stitched down across the width *(Fig. 21)*. The size of the pleats will determine the fullness of the scallops at the bottom as they open out down the length of the fabric. The 15-cm wide pleats should be about 25-30 cm apart, and 30 cm should be added to the finished length of the blind to determine the working drop. The rings through which the cords will pass are sewn to the back of the pleats. Velcro tape is attached across the top of the blind, and the reciprocal strip stapled or glued to a wooden lath. The blind is mounted on the lath and strung in the same way as described for festoon blinds *(Fig. 22)*. Bows or rosettes may be sewn on at the top where the pleats begin.

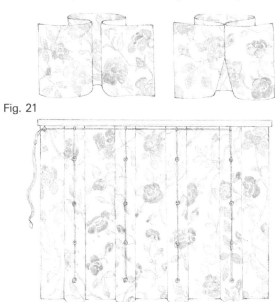

Fig. 21

Fig. 22

15 cm   25-30 cm

ABOVE: Bright yellow bows add a finishing touch to a box blind.
OPPOSITE: A window should be wide enough to accommodate at least two swags on a festoon blind.

London blinds

This is a variation of a pleated festoon blind. Instead of having box pleats across the full width at the top, only two box pleats are formed about 15 cm in on either side of the blind. The depth of each pleat should be approximately 15 cm. Add 30 cm to the finished length to determine the working drop. The rings through which the cording will pass must be sewn to the backs of these two pleats *(Fig. 23)*. The bottom edge of the blind is left unadorned and forms a single soft scallop which is held in place by the cording when the blind is fully lowered (p. 63, step 15). When the blind is raised, the folds of the scallop gather on top of one another to create a draped, swagged effect. Contrasting piping right round the blind adds a decorative finishing touch.

Fig. 23

ABOVE: Filtered sunlight creates a harmony of shadow and light on the sculpted swag at the bottom of the London blind.
LEFT: The London blind is corded through the rings and screw eyes in the same way as a festoon blind.

Balloon blinds

This blind combines the plainness of a Roman blind with the soft fullness of a festoon blind. It is similar to a Roman blind in that a flat rectangular piece of fabric is used. Instead of pulling into concertina pleats, however, the blind is only corded on the two sides, 5 cm in from the edge *(Fig. 24)*. Extra fabric is allowed along the length which drapes into a single soft scallop at the base when the blind is lowered. This scallop is held in position by the cording (p63, step 15). When the blind is raised, this scallop becomes more exaggerated to create a 'ballooning' effect *(Fig. 25)*. A wooden batten is inserted into a casing at the bottom to add weight and to prevent the blind curling in.

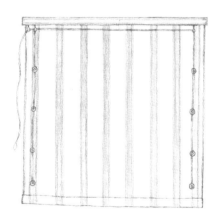

Fig. 24

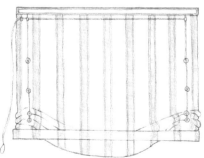

Fig. 25

ABOVE: Soft scallops fold on top of one another as this plain balloon blind is raised.

LEFT: These illustrations show how a balloon blind is corded and the 'ballooning' effect created when the cords are pulled.

USEFUL ADDRESSES

UNITED KINGDOM

The following companies stock extensive ranges of fabric and trimmings suitable for all types of window-dressing. Most will also make curtains and blinds to order, and give advice on the choice of fabrics and on making your own soft furnishings. (Many – for example Laura Ashley – have nationwide outlets.)

Laura Ashley
35 Bow Street
London WC2E 7AU
(071)-240-1997

Michael J Bracey
35-37 Alma Vale Road
Clifton
Bristol B58 2HS
(0272)-734-664

Claremont Furnishing
Fabrics Ltd
12 Kingly Street
London W1R 5LD
(071)-437-5502

Colefax & Fowler
39 Brook Street
London W1Y 2JE
(071)-493-2231

Deans Blinds
Unit 4
Haselmere Industrial Estate
Ravensbury Terrace
London SW13 4SE
(081)-947-8931

Decor (Aberdeen) Ltd
157 Skeen Street
Aberdeen AB1 1QL
(0224)-64-6533

Designers Guild
277 Kings Road
London SW3 5EN
(071)-351-5775

Distinctive Trimmings
17A Kensington Church Street
London W8 4LF
(071)-937-6174

AF Drysdale
35 North West Circus Place
Edinburgh EH3 6TW
(031)-225-4686

Habitat Designs Ltd
195 Finchley Road
London NW3 6NW
(071)-328-3444

Harrison Drape
PO Box 233
Bradford Street
Birmingham B12 0PE
(021)-766-6111

Heal's
196 Tottenham Court Road
London W1P 9LD
(071)-636-1666

John Lewis Partnership
278-306 Oxford Street
London W1A 1EX
(071)-629-7711

Liberty Retail Ltd
210-220 Regent Street
London W1R 6AH
(071)-734-1234

Marvic Textiles Ltd
12-14 Mortimer Street
London W1N 7RD
(071)-580-7951

Osborne and Little
304 King's Road
London SW3 5UH
(071)-352-1456

Paine & Co
49 Barnsbury Street
London N1 1TP
(071)-607-1176

Roomours Design Ltd
28-32 Winchcombe Street
Cheltenham
Glos GL52 2LY
(0242)-52-1155

Russell and Chapple
23 Monmouth Street
London WC2H 9DE
(071)-836-7521

Arthur Sanderson & Sons
53 Berners Street
London W1P 3AD
(071)-636-7800

Warner Fabrics
7 Noel Street
London W1V 4AL
(071)-439-2411

A complete list of UK fabric outlets is available from:

West End Furnishing Fabrics
Association
Stransky Thompson PR
26 Lloyd Baker Street
London WC1X 9AU
071-833-3373

AUSTRALIA

Laura Ashley
114 Castlereagh Street
Sydney
New South Wales
(010612)-261-2458

BIBLIOGRAPHY

Caprice Australia Ltd
14 Wren Road
Moorabbin
Victoria
(010612)-555-9233

Decortex Wall Covering &
Fabrics
(010612)-663-0531

John Glynn
Design House
28 Latrobe Terrace
Brisbane
Queensland
(010617)-368-3844

Piaff Living
29 Ranelagh Drive
Mount Eliza
Victoria
(010613)-787-7336

Trak Accessories
12 Arden Court
Bentleigh
Victoria
(010613)-579-5555

NEW ZEALAND

Curtain Textiles Furniture Ltd
Box 1265
Rotorua 13783
North Island
(01064)-7-348-9979

Draper Warehouse Ltd
Box 9090
Auckland 1295
North Island
(01064)-9-524-8369

Nesbitt Furnishings
Box 10039
Wellington 2944
North Island
(01064)-4-568-5822

Windoware Products Ltd
Box 9025
Christchurch 8588
South Island
(01064)-3-366-9810

Publications on all aspects of interior decoration and soft furnishings abound; the following will provide useful additional information.

Clifton-Mogg, C. 1985. *The Habitat Home Decorator – Curtains and Blinds*. London, Conran Octopus.

Clifton-Mogg, C. and Paine, M., 1988. *The Curtain Book*. London, Mitchell Beazley.

Designers Guild, 1980. *Soft Furnishings*. London, Pan Books.

Dickson, E. and Colvin, M., 1982. *The Laura Ashley Book of Home Decorating*. London, Conran Octopus.

Kittier, E., 1986. *Curtains and Blinds*. London, Ward Lock.

Paine, M., 1987. *Fabric Magic*. London, Frances Lincoln.

Watts, C., 1986. *Cushions, Curtains and Blinds*. London, Macdonald Orbis.

Wilde, E., 1988, *Laura Ashley Windows*. London, Weidenfeld & Nicolson.

INDEX